A River to Cross

The History of the Dartmouth Ferries

By

David Stranack

Dartmouth History Research Group

ISBN 1 899011 21 8

FOREWORD

At a meeting of the Dartmouth History Research Group in the summer of 2001 it was mentioned that it had long been an ambition of the Group to produce a booklet on the history of the town's ferries. But up to that time no-one had been prepared to take on the role of author. With the naïvety that comes from being a relatively new member of a group, I volunteered.

The project turned out to be fascinating, and actually not particularly difficult. There is no shortage of historical information about the ferries and I was fortunate to uncover some very useful sources at an early stage.

However, it did not appear that this information had ever been drawn together into a single document covering all three ferries - so this is what this book attempts to do.

Many people have contributed, directly or indirectly, to the compilation of this chronicle and to all of them I owe a debt of gratitude.

Ferries have been an integral part of Dartmouth life for many centuries in the past and will continue to be so for many more centuries to come.

I hope you enjoy reading about them.

David Stranack
Strete, Devon
Spring 2002

CONTENTS

LIST OF ILLUSTRATIONS

INTRODUCTION

From the beginning of time man has been fascinated by water – and even more fascinated by what lies "on the other side" of the water. Brave seafarers have set out towards distant horizons, not knowing when they will find "the other side", or what they will encounter when they get there.

When the other side is only three hundred yards away, the adventure is less daunting. So it was probably some of our very earliest ancestors that stood on the banks of the river Dart and contemplated a crossing. They would have only needed the most basic of craft – perhaps no more than a tree trunk and an improvised paddle – to achieve their objective. But once the feasibility of this venture had been established, it wouldn't have been long before one of our more nervous ancestors asked one of the braver ones – "Can you take me across?" – and the first ferry service would have been born.

Significant settlements on the banks of the Dart, where Dartmouth and Kingswear stand today, probably didn't become established until late in the eleventh century. Neither name appears in the Domesday survey of 1086, although Townstal, on the hill above Dartmouth, does. Before this time, dwelling close to a river that had easy access to the sea was not considered to be particularly important, and might even have been dangerous. In addition, the steep hills on both banks made travelling to and from the river difficult. Good farming land on high ground with less severe slopes was the preferred place to live.

But the influence of the Normans, following their invasion of England in 1066, gradually began to change attitudes. They appreciated how the use of ships, both on the open sea and on inland rivers, could facilitate trade – and the lower reaches of the river Dart provided a marvellous natural harbour. Increasingly, some of the inhabitants of Townstal began to see the advantages of living closer to the river – at the mouth of the Dart – and it cannot have been long before their settlement was referred to as Dart Mouth.

On the other side of the river it is likely that a similar migration was taking place. People living in inland villages such as Kingston and Woodhuish would have made their way along the banks of Waterhead creek to build dwellings at Kittery Point, and start the community that was to become Kingswear.

As more and more people settled on both sides of the river, there would have been increasing needs for them to communicate and meet. They had a stark choice. A twenty mile round trip via Totnes, on foot or on horseback, or a three hundred yard trip across the water. It is little wonder that river ferries have been a major feature of the life of this area from the earliest days.

Today there are three ferry services operating between Dartmouth and the Kingswear side of the river.

The Lower Ferry, carrying both vehicles and pedestrians, is by far the oldest, and has been operating on basically the same route between Bayards Cove and Kingswear for hundreds of years.

The Higher Ferry, or floating bridge, provides a link between the roads at Sandquay on the west bank, and Lower Noss Point on the east. Its design is unusual, but not unique. It is a paddle wheel driven platform, guided across the river on steel hawsers. Although today the paddles are driven by a powerful diesel engine, the basic engineering concept of this ferry has not otherwise changed very much since it started life in 1831.

The third and most recent ferry is the one which carries foot passengers from the pontoon off the Embankment on the Dartmouth side to a similar pontoon by Kingswear station. Today this ferry provides a quick and convenient way of crossing the river for locals and tourists alike. But when it was introduced in 1864 it had a very specific purpose. It was the Railway Ferry, and it was the means by which passengers arriving by train at Kingswear completed the last leg of their journey to Dartmouth.

To some extent the histories of these ferries, particularly the Lower Ferry and the Railway Ferry, are interlinked. But any attempt to produce a single consolidated history of all three ferries would have resulted in an overly complex and confusing tale. So the story of each is told separately, starting with the oldest.

THE LOWER FERRIES

In 1365 the records of the Court of Chancery – known as the Close Rolls – make mention of a ferry across the River Dart. The ferry was established as a "monopoly" by the Crown which ensured that the service would be provided on a continuous basis.

The court documents show that in 1365 William Carey acquired the rights to operate the ferry from Martin de Fishacre. The costs of operating and maintaining the ferry in those days were probably recouped by way of a tithe imposed upon local landowners.

This assumption is reinforced by the records of 1544 which document the purchase of the Manor of Kingswear by Thomas Gale. As the new owner of the manor he was obliged to contribute ten shillings and four pence ha'penny each year to the upkeep of the ferry service.

The owner of the ferry rights would normally contract out the actual operation of the ferry to a tenant, and in 1558 – the same year as the first Queen Elizabeth came to the throne - Robert Collyns was the tenant for life, paying a rental of twelve shillings a year, which also included half the landing stage.

Almost certainly this landing stage was at Kittery Point on the Kingswear side of the river, which to this day bears the name of Collins Quay. John Leland writes in about 1540: " I ferid over to Kingswear. This town standeth on a pointlet into the haven." Bayards Cove, or Bearscove as it was previously known, would have been the landing point on the Dartmouth side. This route, traversing one of the narrowest parts of the river, had probably been where the earliest ferries started – and of course is still in use today.

In these days the ferry would have been a simple boat rowed by a single oarsmen. It was known as the "pulling ferry".

A River to Cross

By the 17th century all the hamlets in the parish of Brixham were required to contribute "passage money" to the owner of the ferry rights, and it seems likely that this generated a useful source of income for the owner which probably substantially exceeded the costs of operating the service.

At this time the ferry rights were held jointly by the Holway family and the Mallock family of Cockington.

The information that exists about the ferry during this period of history often relates to the important people who made use of it. On the 23rd July 1671 King Charles II arrived in Dartmouth by sea. He was lavishly entertained by local dignitaries in the Butterwalk, and was then ferried across to Kingswear to continue his journey to Exeter by road.

In 1691 the ferry was used for a more sombre purpose. John Flavel, the Puritan minister and a Dartmothian of considerable note, died on his way to a religious meeting in Topsham. His body was brought back to Kingswear by his mourning followers, and was carried across the river by the ferry to Dartmouth where he was buried in the chancel of St. Saviour's church.

During the 17th and 18th centuries changes were taking place on the Kingswear side of the river. In 1717 John Fownes bought the Manor of Kingswear, and subsequently he also purchased many of the properties in the village. This changed the nature of Kingswear from being a busy little port, which it had been previously, to a much more residential area.

This could have been one of the reasons why, about this time, a new ferry service began operating from Hoo Down, on the northern bank of Waterhead Creek. This ran across to the New Ground at Dartmouth, which was land reclaimed from the river between 1670 and 1680.

It could also have been that Hoo Down was easier to get to by road for travellers on the eastern side of the Dart, rather than continuing on around the top of Waterhead creek into Kingswear itself.

Although this new ferry – which came to be known as the Hoo

Down Passage – probably started operating in the first part of the 18th century, there is one piece of evidence that suggests its commencement may have been even earlier. John Ogilvy writing in 1675 says " you ferry over the Dart (three furlongs in width here) and on the other side pass through a village of about two furlongs extent." Three furlongs is 660 yards which is twice the distance between Collins Quay and Bayards Cove, and approximates much more closely to the journey between Hoo Down and the New Ground. So it seems likely that Mr. Ogilvy could have been one of the Hoo Down ferry's earliest passengers.

Meanwhile the original pulling ferry continued to operate on the shorter Kingswear to Dartmouth crossing, but in the main was only used by local people.

An inn was built at Hoo Down to provide weary travellers with rest and sustenance. The inn seemed to acquire a number of names during its lifetime – the Passage House Inn, the Hoo Down Ferry House, and just the Ferry Inn – but there is little more information recorded about it. It is known that Mary Burgoyne was the inn keeper in 1863. She had married James Fleet, the ferryman in 1856, but presumably chose to continue using her maiden name. The census of 1881 shows her still in residence.

The inn did, however, outlive the ferry itself, as it was not demolished until 1927, whereas the ferry ceased operation in 1864 with the coming of the railway.

Until 1863 both the Hoo Down and Kingswear ferries were owned by the Fownes-Luttrell family. Henry Fownes, the elder grandson of John, had married Margaret Luttrell, the heiress to Dunster Castle in Somerset, in 1747. They had adopted Fownes-Luttrell as the family name, and were now major landowners in the area.

For a long time there was no provision for wheeled vehicles – carts and wagons – to cross the river. The little rowing boats could accommodate foot passengers only. But in 1840 the Fownes-Luttrells responded to the increasing demand and introduced a larger float, rowed by two men with very long oars, or "sweeps", which could carry one horse drawn wagon at a time. This became known as the Horse Ferry, although, in view of the continued existence of the Hoo Down Passage at that time, it was also often referred to by locals as the Lower Ferry – as indeed it is today.

For a large part of the nineteenth century the operation of the ferry was closely associated with the Plume of Feathers inn on the Kingswear side of the river. The Exeter Flying Post of 7th February 1805 offered the public house and the ferry, together, "… to be let for a term of 7 to 14 years". In the early 1850s a Mr. Cox was fulfilling the dual role of publican and ferry operator, but in March 1855 both jobs were taken over by Mr. Sandover. It seems as if Mr. Cox may not have been the most diligent of ferrymen because at the time of Mr. Sandover's arrival the newly established Dartmouth Chronicle commented on the previous deficiencies of the ferry service, and expressed the hope that "… the ferry will be conducted with more regard to the public". It is likely that Mr. Sandover continued to be responsible for the operation of the ferry until 1865.

But by now developments were being discussed that would eventually have a major impact on the river's ferry services. It was proposed that the railway line that already ran from Exeter to Newton Abbott should be extended to Kingswear, and in 1857 the Dartmouth and Torbay Railway Company was formed to take this project forward. In the event, the building of the railway line took much longer, and was vastly more expensive than anyone had originally envisaged. It was first intended to terminate the line at Hoo Down, from where the ferry across to Dartmouth already operated. But then it was decided that the trains would continue on across Waterhead creek to a terminus in Kingswear itself. This extension of the line required land to be rented from the Fownes-Luttrell family, and at the same time it was agreed that the family would sell the rights of both ferries – Hoo Down and the Lower Ferry – to the railway company as well.

In 1864 the long awaited railway was at last opened. With trains now running through to Kingswear, it was decided that the Hoo Down Passage was redundant and it was closed down, after nearly 200 years of operation.

Dartmouth and Torbay Railway Company were now the owners of both the Lower Ferry, and the new passenger ferry service they had set up, primarily for railway travellers, which operated from pontoons on both sides of the river.

Soon after the railway company acquired the rights to the Lower Ferry its operation was leased to Messrs Avis and Son of Kingswear. The parliamentary act which set up the railway also gave the Postmaster General considerable powers to order the ferry operators to carry mail across the river to Dartmouth. Fines could be imposed for any failure to meet these obligations. However, as Mr. Avis was also the local postmaster, and therefore the representative of the Postmaster General, it is unlikely that he fined himself for any shortcomings in his ferry service.

At this time three boats were used to provide the ferry service between Kingswear and Bayards Cove – two rowing boats, for foot passengers only, and a new "horse boat" to carry both wagons and luggage. This new vessel, supplied by the railway company, could take one wagon with a four ton load, together with two horses, and it could be loaded and unloaded from either end. At first it was still propelled across the river by two oarsmen, but in 1867 steam power was introduced with the arrival of *Pioneer*. Built by J. Samuel White of Cowes to the order of Mr. Avis, she was 30 feet in length, and capable of eight knots – an impressive vessel by the standards of the day. Her maiden voyage from the Isle of Wight to the Dart was, however, somewhat less impressive. On departing from Cowes she ran into heavy weather, and had to run for shelter in Weymouth harbour. In doing so she was unfortunate enough to strike an unmarked rock, and suffered extensive damage as a result. Repairs were made, but it was decided not to complete the rest of the journey by sea, and eventually *Pioneer* made a rather ignominious arrival at her new home port on the back of a railway wagon.

Nevertheless, *Pioneer* enabled Mr. Avis to provide a considerably improved ferry service. It was claimed that she could cross the river with the horse boat in 3 ¼ minutes, and on her own, with up to thirty passengers on board, she could do the journey in half that time.

In October of the same year further improvements were made to the slipway on the Kingswear side, and a small quay was added to make it easier for passengers to board the ferry at high tide.

Mr. Avis' original lease from the railway company expired in June 1877, and operation of the ferry was then taken on by two brothers – George and John Casey – who came from a long-established Kingswear family. They were initially granted a five year lease at a cost of £73 per annum, but this was just the beginning of the Casey family's involvement with the Lower Ferry, an era which was to continue for nearly fifty years.

The change of responsibility for operating the ferry sparked off local interest, and the Chronicle announced – "Messrs Casey will take possession from Monday next of the Lower Ferry, and in lieu of the usual rowing boats run a steam launch taking passengers to and from all trains during winter and summer. A steam launch is now in the course of construction to be put on the service, thus affording better accommodation".

The Casey's assumed responsibility for the ferry on 25th June 1877, and immediately introduced their new launch, *Blanche*, which they had purchased for £165. No mention is made of the 10-year-old *Pioneer* at this time, so she may have already been pensioned off, or she may have been working exclusively on the horse boat. In any case, the immediate improvements to the ferry service were much appreciated locally, and the Chronicle was moved to comment that "...we trust Messrs Casey will receive the support their spirit and energy so deserves".

In addition to *Blanche,* another new steam launch was ordered, and constructed by John Houston at his boatyard at Coombe. She was *Forester,* named by the Casey's after the Masonic lodge of which both brothers were members. *Forester* was of similar design to *Pioneer* and was used mainly for driving the horse boat, but she was also used as a passenger launch on occasions as well.

Blanche and *Forester* were the mainstays of the Casey's ferry operations for some years – and indeed *Blanche* was still in operation in

1912 at the age of 35. But in those days the service was not without some degree of unauthorised competition. Unscrupulous boatmen would wait around the slip at Bayard's Cove until the Casey ferry had departed and then offer to take unwary passengers across the river. Once in midstream, they would demand a fee of 4d – against the official price of ½ d – to continue the journey. This practice declined rapidly after one or two outraged passengers took the law into their own hands and dumped the offending boatmen in the river.

By 1896 the Casey's, having run the ferry successfully for nearly twenty years, were beginning to encounter financial difficulties. Income was declining, possibly as a result of increased competition from the Railway Ferry itself, and they asked the railway company – by then the Great Western Railway – if they could be released from their obligations. GWR considered the matter but could find no one else willing to take on the operation of the Lower Ferry, so offered a significantly reduced rental to the Casey's to persuade them to soldier on for another twelve months. During this period business must have picked up again because in May 1897 the Casey brothers committed themselves to a new five year lease which incorporated an increase of more than 50% in the previously agreed annual rental.

John Casey died in 1901, and his role in the partnership was taken on by his son Tom, who was subsequently to become one of Dartmouth's best known ferrymen.

Inevitably minor incidents and accidents occurred from time to time while the ferry was being operated – and many were never recorded for posterity – but in April 1903 a more major near-disaster was reported by the Chronicle. The ketch *Lord Napier* was entering the harbour and proving difficult to handle. She collided with the horse boat, damaging one of the wagons on board, and creating panic among the horses. The vessel was eventually detached from the ferry and progressed further upstream where she also managed to collide with the floating bridge. She finally ran aground at Noss, and remained stuck there for several days.

1909 saw the death of George Casey, and his nephew, Tom, took on Mr. F.C. Heal as his partner. They ordered a new tug from Philip's shipyard. She was called *Hauley,* a name that is still used by the ferry tugs today. (The first river Dart tug bearing the name *Hauley* was actually built in 1877, but she was not involved in ferry work.)

For hundreds of years travellers had relied upon the strong arms of oarsmen to row them across the river Dart. This tradition finally came to an end in 1915 when the last pulling ferry was replaced by a steam launch, *Edna.* The new service was no doubt quicker and more efficient, but many locals commented on how much they missed the cheery banter of the old ferrymen. *Edna* in fact only operated for a few months before she was herself replaced by *Relief,* a new, much larger launch that could carry up to 25 passengers.

But *Relief's* initial involvement in the ferry service was itself short-lived. The Great War was beginning to have an impact on many aspects of life in England. So many men were being thrown into the battle in France that there was a severe shortage of manpower at home. All three of Dartmouth's ferries were affected, and *Relief* had to be laid up as there were just not sufficient experienced boatmen available to man her.

The end of the war heralded a period of change for the Lower Ferry. Casey and Heal had concluded that some of the obligations placed upon them by the lease they held from the railway company, GWR, were too onerous. They asked the railway if it would agree to the discontinuation of the ferry service on Sundays. With some reluctance GWR acceded to this request, albeit on a temporary basis, but it is likely that this relatively minor negotiation between the two parties was the starting point of the railway company rethinking its ferry strategy. It was at the time paying considerable sums of money to Casey and Heal to transport its own parcel delivery vehicles across to Dartmouth. So GWR set about trying to reduce both its costs, and its dependence on the Lower Ferry. It decided to experiment with using its own Railway Ferry boat, *The Mew,* to carry vehicles as well as foot passengers. *The Mew* was suitably adapted, and the pontoons on both sides of the river were strengthened so that vehicles could be loaded and unloaded.

The experiment was a success, and as a result a significant part of the vehicle traffic shifted from the Lower Ferry to the Railway Ferry. GWR recognised this by reducing the rental paid by Casey and Heal for the Lower Ferry from £85 to £50 per annum, and renewed their lease in 1922 for a further 3 years.

But the writing was already on the wall. GWR was increasingly happy with the operation of its Railway Ferry and began to view the Lower Ferry as an irrelevance. When Casey and Heal's lease came to an end in 1925, it was not renewed. Whether the railway refused to renew it, or whether the new terms it proposed were unacceptable, is not clear. In October, the Casey dynasty – 48 years of involvement with the Lower Ferry - finally came to an end.

There was no doubt that Tom Casey felt disgruntled about the way he had been dealt with by GWR. Motivated perhaps more by pique than by sound financial judgement, he set up his own private ferry service in competition. Using his 12-seater launch, *I'll Try,* he plied between Gibbs Steps on the Kingswear side across to Bayards Cove, but he found it difficult to make a profit and gave up after ten months.

Tom Casey was one of Dartmouth's best know ferryman – one of the great characters of the river. He died in 1976 at the age of 94, having lived all his life in Kingswear. To this day, one of the Lower Ferry floats, launched in 1989, carries his name.

There was sadness locally at GWR's ousting of the Casey and Heal partnership, but this quickly turned to outrage when it became clear that the railway had no intention of appointing an alternative operator. After hundreds of years of service, the Lower Ferry closed.

There was a public outcry, and a determined campaign was mounted to have the ferry reinstated. The Chronicle speculated that, with the loss of the old horse ferry, passengers would have to mingle with livestock on *The Mew,* which by then was the only large boat operating between Dartmouth and Kingswear.

1. The Lower Ferry crossing with a heavy load in the 1890s.
The steam tug is on the far side, hidden from view.

2. The steam launch, *Blanche*, guiding the Lower Ferry float, with William Casey supervising on the prow.

3. *Relief* guides the Lower Ferry on to the Kingswear slip. Note the somewhat primitive barriers.

4. The Lower Ferry in 1928 with St. Petrox church and Dartmouth Castle in the background.

GWR was forced to take notice, but it had lost its enthusiasm for ownership of the Lower Ferry. Dartmouth Corporation on the other hand felt obliged to make some response to the clamour of the townspeople. Sir Felix Pole, GWR's chairman, was invited to visit Dartmouth. It is rumoured that he was well wined and dined by the Corporation, but whether this is true or not, he agreed to transfer ownership of the Lower Ferry to the Corporation for a nominal sum of £100, plus a fee of £5 per annum for the use of the slipways.

The Corporation promptly invited tenders for the operation of the ferry service, but only received two responses. One was a blank one from Tom Casey, still smarting from the way he had been treated, and the other was from a Mr. Peters and a Mrs. Blanche Heseltine of Kingswear. Mr. Peters had recently been a partner in the firm Peters and Raymond, coal merchants of Bayards Cove. Their offer of £250 per annum for 14 years was accepted, and much to the relief of the locals the Lower Ferry commenced operation again the following year, having been out of action for ten months. The original tug *Hauley* continued to be used, together with the two elderly wooden horse ferry floats, all acquired from GWR.

In 1929, three years into their lease, the Peters Heseltine partnership was confronted with its first serious mishap when the tug propelling the float suffered engine failure in mid-stream and the whole ensemble began drifting out to sea on the ebb tide. It was eventually recovered well past Warfleet Creek – much to the relief of the passengers on board.

In the same year it became apparent that the two old floats, originally designed to carry horses and carts, were becoming completely inadequate to cope with the growing number of motor vehicles crossing the river. The ferry owners, Dartmouth Corporation, ordered a new purpose built float capable of carrying eight cars, which soon acquired the nickname *Big Jumbo*. This commenced operation in July, but it quickly became apparent that the increased weight and size of the new float was more than the old tug *Hauley* could handle. The Corporation suggested that a permanent solution to this problem could be achieved by running the Lower

Ferry across the river on guide wires, in identical fashion to the Higher Ferry. However, the prospect of having ferry wires dangling in the water across the busiest part of the port almost induced apoplexy in the office of the Harbour Commission, and the idea progressed no further. So a new, more powerful tug was commissioned from Percy Mitchell, shipbuilders of Portmellon. She was named *Hauley I,* and took up station the following year.

The passenger launch, *Relief,* was also coming to the end of her days after fourteen years continuous service, and she was replaced by *Perseverance,* built by Ferris and Blank at Coombe. (She was the second Dartmouth ferry to be named *Perseverance.* The first vessel had been used on the Railway Ferry between 1864 and 1869.)

An order for *Hauley II* was placed by the Peters and Heseltine partnership in 1932, but by then Peters, who had always been the active partner, was beginning to extend his business interests elsewhere. He offered to sell the remainder of his lease back to Dartmouth Corporation for £12000. He subsequently reduced this figure to £8000, but this was still much more than the Corporation was prepared to pay, and Peters eventually sold the lease to General Estates Co Ltd of Bond Street, London – for an undisclosed sum.

It is not known whether General Estates had previous experience of running ferry services, or indeed how closely the company was actually involved in the day to day operations, but the Lower Ferry ran reasonably efficiently under its ownership for seventeen years. New boats were introduced – *Hauley III* in 1933, and *Reliance,* a new 35 foot passenger launch built by Lavers of South Town in 1936.

Inevitably there was the odd mishap as well. On Whit Monday in 1935 the Admiralty yacht *Enchantress* collided with the ferry. The float, which was fortunately only one of the old wooden spares, sank immediately in deep water, but the chargehand, who was the only person on board at the time, was successfully rescued from the river. A second float was lost the following year when it sank by the Dartmouth slip, and in 1937 there was a more dramatic incident when a float with a car and several passengers on board broke loose from its accompanying tug and drifted on to rocks by Warfleet, but fortunately both the float and its payload were eventually recovered unharmed.

In 1947 *Reliance* was replaced with a new launch of the same name.

General Estates lease of the ferry expired on 25th March 1949. It doesn't seem that its renewal or extension was even considered by the Corporation, and there were strong local rumours that the ferry was to close down. But perhaps the Corporation had learnt its lesson in 1925. They decided to take over the running of the ferry themselves, and thus ensure the continuity of the service. The tugs and floats were purchased from General Estates, and a Ferry Committee appointed to oversee operations. There was much relief locally, but this was short-lived when it was learnt that the Corporation intended to double the passenger fee from 1d to 2d.

The new operators were soon confronted with the realities of running ferries when they were accused by Kingswear Parish Council of failing to comply with their own rules – obligatory for all other river boats – regarding lifesaving and fire-fighting equipment. It was recognised that some money needed to be spent. *Perseverance* was 21 years old and barely seaworthy, having to be beached frequently for patching up. And *Reliance,* although much newer, was proving troublesome and had been beached for repairs for some time. A new launch, *Newcomen,* was ordered from Blackmore's of Bideford to replace *Perseverance,* and the quality of the ferry service improved.

The 1950s were a time of change for the river's ferry services. The Lower ferry discontinued its passenger launches, and became primarily a car ferry, while its neighbour up stream – The Railway Ferry – provided the main service for those travelling on foot.

But fifty years on, as a new century begins, there still exists much that the old ferrymen would find familiar. The floats are still pushed, pulled and manoeuvred across the river by tugs, which still carry the familiar

Hauley name. The two present vessels are *Hauley V*, with over thirty years of service to her credit, and *Hauley VI*, a mere youngster of eleven.

But perhaps Tom Casey would be a bit surprised to learn that the Lower Ferry is now run by a staff of fourteen people, and costs about £500,000 a year to operate.

Life on the ferries is demanding, and can even be dangerous. Bob Floyd, a ferryman in the nineteen eighties, finished his last crossing one night, and then set off on his own to moor up the ferry float to its buoy in the middle of the river. Nobody knows for certain what happened on that last trip, but Bob was never seen again.

So often the river looks idyllic and benign. But it is not always so. Imagine a dark winter night, a rapidly ebbing spring tide, and a fog so thick that you can't see the lights on either bank. Good conditions to be tucked up in bed. But the ferryman is out there, using his skill and dedication to carry his passengers safely from shore to shore.

THE RAILWAY FERRY

When the building of Dartmouth station was completed in 1889 it was unique. It was the only railway station in England that had no lines, no platforms – and no trains.

The middle of the nineteenth century was a time of rapid expansion for England's railway systems. By the early 1850s the main line from London to Exeter was well established, and had been extended to Newton Abbott. The question was – where next?

The ports of Dartmouth and Kingswear were obvious choices. One early suggestion was to bring the railway direct to Dartmouth via a bridge over the Dart just below Dittisham, using the Anchor Stone as a central support. This proposal was progressed to the point of being debated in the House of Lords – where it was rejected.

Running the line down the eastern bank of the river seemed to be a more acceptable idea, and the Dartmouth and Torbay Railway Bill was drafted to obtain the necessary parliamentary approval for this project. The Bill was duly passed by both Houses, and received the Royal Assent in 1857.

The original plan was to terminate the railway line at Hoo Down, on the northern side of Waterhead creek. But it was soon decided that the extension of the line to a station in Kingswear itself would be more satisfactory. With the terminus at Kingswear, there was a danger that Dartmouth would become the poor relation in terms of railway services, so the Act made it quite clear that Dartmouth too would have a station. It wouldn't have any trains, but there would be a ticket office and waiting room, and porters would be on hand to help passengers with their luggage. Perhaps most importantly, the Act made specific provision for a ferry service to be operated between Kingswear and the station at Dartmouth, and also for the construction of the necessary piers, pontoons and landing places on both sides of the river.

Dartmouth thus acquired its third ferry.

However, not everybody was enthusiastic about this scheme. The Higher Ferry, or floating bridge, which ran across the river further upstream from Sandquay on the Dartmouth side, belonged to local landowner and businessman, Sir Henry Seale. It had commenced operation in 1831, almost thirty years earlier, but had struggled financially ever since.

The 1857 Railway Act authorised the creation of the Dartmouth and Torbay Railway Co, and it also gave this company the right to purchase the Higher Ferry. In spite of the financial problems, Sir Henry was not keen to relinquish the ownership of his ferry, but could foresee even greater problems arising from the increased competition the new Railway Ferry would create. However, he held a trump card. It was necessary for the railway line to cross the Higher Ferry road – which Sir Henry also owned – on the eastern bank of the river. He obtained a court injunction which not only prohibited the railway from crossing his road, but also forbade any new ferry service commencing operation within three miles of the floating bridge. The Railway Company realised it had a problem. Its solution was to offer Sir Henry a seat on its board plus £2000 to ensure his co-operation. In addition, the company surrendered its right to buy the floating bridge. Not surprisingly, Sir Henry was satisfied, and withdrew his injunction.

The chairman of the new Railway Company was Charles Seale-Hayne, Sir Henry's nephew. It may therefore seem that an element of nepotism was at work here, but in fact there was always a degree of antipathy between these two business men from the same family, mainly because of their strong disagreements over politics.

Charles Seale-Hayne undoubtedly had a sharp eye for a business opportunity. When the time came for his Railway Company to grant a lease for the operation of the new ferry service, he promptly formed the Dartmouth Steam Packet Co – to whom the lease was awarded!

It took seven years to build the Kingswear line – much longer than originally anticipated. The construction of the track was completed during the first half of 1864, and the Railway Company decided to go ahead with the official opening in August that year, even though much of the rest of the infrastructure was unfinished. Kingswear station was still being built, and on the Dartmouth side the station was no more than a temporary building on a pontoon. What's more, the vessel destined to be the first Railway Ferry, *Perseverance,* was still undergoing overhaul and conversion. So it was decided that *Newcomen,* a boat launched the previous June, and the eight year old *Louisa* would operate the ferry service until such time as *Perseverance* was ready.

On the 10th August the first train, loaded with Railway Company directors and other dignitaries, puffed its ceremonious way from Brixham Road station to Kingswear to declare the line officially open. *Newcomen,* even though she had had to be substantially modified in the first two months of her life, was chosen to transport the VIP passengers across the river to the New Ground. There they were surrounded by cheering crowds, and greeted by the Mayor of Dartmouth – none other than Sir Henry Seale – and the Corporation.

So the railway and its ferry became part of every day life in Dartmouth and Kingswear. The work on *Perseverance* was carried out by Lewis and Stockwell of Thameside, who had also built *Newcomen.* It was not finally completed until the autumn, and she commenced operation on the 1st October 1864. Problems soon arose, and she was off station again from March to May the following year for further work on her machinery and boilers. *Louisa* was once again drafted in as a temporary replacement.

The Railway Company had originally expected that *Perseverance* would cost about £800, but were confronted with much larger bills from Lewis and Stockwell. Eventually an independent arbitrator had to be brought in to settle the dispute, and a figure of £1799-13s-8d was agreed.

Apart from her mechanical problems, the basic design of *Perseverance* was not well suited to river ferry work. She was a 60 ton paddle steamer with double-ended steering, and was not particularly easy to handle, especially in high winds. In 1868, shortly after she had been off station again for a period of seven months, the inevitable happened. She set off across the river before sufficient steam had been raised to give the engines full power. The captain lost control of the vessel in mid stream, and she collided with a coal lighter, which sank. The irate owners of the lighter took the Railway Company to court, and won their case.

By now the Dartmouth and Torbay Railway Company had been absorbed into the South Devon Railway, and perhaps it was this change of management that concluded that *Perseverance's* days were numbered. In any case, by the end of 1868 a new purpose built vessel had been ordered from Messrs Harvey of Hayle, and was under construction. She was *Dolphin,* designed, whether advisedly or not, by the railway's Locomotive Superintendent, Mr. Wright. The vessel was a 105 foot double-ended paddle steamer, which could carry up to 331 passengers across the river in four minutes. But somewhat surprisingly – and presumably to save cost – a decision was taken to remove the much repaired engines and boiler from *Perseverance,* overhaul them yet again, and install them in *Dolphin.*

Nevertheless, *Dolphin,* having commenced operations on 24th August 1869 managed to provide a relatively satisfactory and uneventful service for four years. But in 1873 her engine problems recurred, and she had to be fitted with a new boiler at a cost of £500. By then the South Devon Railway had decided to take over the running of the ferry themselves, rather than contracting it out to the Steam Packet Company, although the latter was still required to provide a replacement boat while *Dolphin* was out of action. *Dolphin,* with her new boiler fitted, returned to the river in September, but only ran trouble free for a little over a year. In January 1875 she was off station again awaiting the installation of new engines, her owners presumably having given up hope of squeezing further life out of those originally installed in *Perseverance.*

It does seem that the decision to install second hand engines in *Dolphin* when she was originally being built, did blight her early life on the Dart. Once she had new engines of her own she proved to be a very satisfactory vessel, and continued operating the ferry service until she was replaced in 1908, after nearly forty years of service.

In 1876 management of the South Devon line was taken over by the Great Western Railway (GWR), and they promptly reversed the decision, taken four years earlier, to run the ferry service themselves. A new 25 year lease was awarded to the Steam Packet Company which once again assumed responsibility for day to day operations. They also took over ownership of *Dolphin,* and continued to use her as their main vessel.

As the twentieth century dawned, *Dolphin* had been in operation for 31 years, and it was decided that she no longer met the contemporary standards for passenger comfort. She was withdrawn from service for substantial refurbishment and "modernisation". This included the addition of a glazed saloon on deck, which soon acquired the nickname of the "cucumber frame" among local passengers.

If *Dolphin* were off station for any reason, the Steam Packet Company were obliged to provide a replacement vessel. The paddle steamers *Berry Castle, Dartmouth Castle,* and *Totnes Castle* were all required to fulfil this role from time to time, and it was in 1901, when *Totnes Castle* was on temporary duty, that a near disaster occurred. She was crossing from Kingswear with a full load of passengers and caught the hawser holding the collier *SS Celeste* to No. 3 buoy. Her mast, funnel, ventilators and steering wheel were all swept overboard. There was panic among the passengers, especially as Captain Fleet, the skipper, nearly followed the bits of his boat into the river. But he eventually managed to bring the vessel alongside the Embankment, and everybody on board was safely disembarked.

In the same year, the Steam Packet Company's lease of the ferry expired, and the Railway, in the form of GWR, made yet another U turn. They decided once again to run the ferry service themselves, and declined to renew the lease.

The venerable *Dolphin* finally had her moment of glory on 7th March 1902. On this day King Edward VII and Queen Alexandra visited Dartmouth to lay the foundation stone of the Britannia Royal Naval College. The plan was for their majesties to travel to Kingswear on the royal train, be transported across the river on *Dolphin,* and then process in their landaus – especially brought to Dartmouth for the occasion – up the hill to the site of the college. Preparations were being made for weeks before the visit as the level of excited anticipation rose. *Dolphin* was taken off station so she could be made fit for her duty as a royal ferry. Her hull and funnel were repainted, and the "cucumber frame" saloon was curtained and carpeted. The usual seating was taken out and replaced with four elegant chairs, two with arms for the king and queen, and two without arms for their aides. Potted plants on stands and an occasional table completed the royal décor. (The furniture was sold two days after the visit in Torquay for £100).

On the 7th March the waiting was finally over. The royal train – renamed Britannia for the day - puffed into Kingswear station, bedecked with flags and bunting, at 2.55 pm, right on schedule. The king and queen walked on a red carpet across the station yard through wildly cheering crowds, and boarded *Dolphin.* As the vessel pulled away from the pontoon the captain, Harry Thorne, ordered the royal standard to be unfurled, and *Dolphin* enjoyed her few minutes of fame as she made her usual crossing, with the most important passengers she had ever carried.

After her participation in the royal visit, *Dolphin* soldiered on for another six years. But as the river became busier and busier it became increasingly apparent that she would eventually need to be replaced. Perhaps this was reinforced by an incident reported in the Chronicle as 1904 drew to a close –

> "The ageing *Dolphin* on Christmas Eve loaded with passengers for the Paddington train had just left Dartmouth pontoon and taking a wide sweep on a strong tide noticed the collier *Vanessa* bearing down on a similar course. As the distance closed, alarm began among the passengers who prepared to jump overboard while the master of the collier, realising that the *Dolphin* had little steerage, screamed through his loud hailer to the *Dolphin* to make full speed ahead which, with the kick of the tide, straightened her up, and the two vessels passed within inches of each other as

5. *Big Jumbo,* the first float purpose built to carry motor vehicles, with the tug *Hauley I.*

6. *Reliance* operating the "Penny Ferry" passenger service in the late 1940s.

7. *Dolphin,* the mainstay of the Railway Ferry service from 1869 to 1908.

8. *The Mew* doing a good trade on the river in 1920.

9. *The Mew* looking very different in 1948 after she had been modified more than once.

10. The people of Dartmouth say farewell to *The Mew* on her last trip – 8th October 1954.

11. *Humphrey Gilbert* carrying passengers across to Kingswear, with the Lower Ferry behind her.

12. An early view of the floating bridge from the Brixham Road, looking across to industrial buildings at Sandquay.

> women fainted and people on Bayards Cove, hearing the pitiful cries, made to launch boats, but a major disaster was just averted."

By 1907 GWR decided that they could delay the issue of *Dolphin's* replacement no longer and ordered a new vessel from the shipbuilders Messrs Cox of Falmouth. She was *The Mew,* and she was destined to become one of the Dart's best known and most loved river boats. Costing £5100, she was a twin screw steamer, 90 feet in length – actually a little shorter than *Dolphin* – but with a broader beam, so she had a maximum passenger carrying capacity of 547, compared with *Dolphin's* 331. Her passenger accommodation was described with some enthusiasm in the GWR magazine of June 1908 –

> "Three deck houses are provided on the main deck, fitted with comfortable seats for the use of passengers during wet or bad weather, and special provision is also made on this deck for the conveyance of passengers' luggage, market goods etc., which are wheeled aboard or ashore in barrows or trolleys and placed under cover while crossing the river. The spacious promenade deck has been kept specially free from obstructions in order to provide ample accommodation for passengers. Captain Pinhey's patent buoyant seats are fitted all around this deck and these form part of the vessel's life saving apparatus required by the Board of Trade. A complete installation of electric lighting is fitted on board."

Before taking over the ferry run from *Dolphin, The Mew* underwent trials on the river, and with a maximum speed of ten knots, and excellent manoeuvrability, she proved to be most satisfactory. So it was on 31st May 1908 that *The Mew* made her inaugural crossing. *Dolphin* was finally decommissioned and towed away to Appledore to be broken up for scrap. Perhaps not many people at that time expected *The Mew* to actually have a longer period of service on the river then *Dolphin's* 39 years.

1908 also saw the death of Captain Thorne, a well known local figure who had skippered *Dolphin* for all her life. He had actually started working on the river in 1864 as a steersman on *Perseverance*, and in later life acquired the nickname of the "Admiral" as a result of his involvement in the royal visit of 1902. Captain Thorne died just four months before his old vessel, *Dolphin,* was consigned to the breaker's yard.

The Mew quickly established herself as an essential and integral part of river life. She worked on through two world wars, and her passenger carrying capacity was used to maximum effect during World War I when she was frequently employed to ferry troops across from their training camp at Dartmouth to board trains at Kingswear en route to France.

In World War II *The Mew* nearly saw action. In June 1940, as the British army retreated to the beaches of Dunkirk, the call went out for any ship that could assist with the evacuation to make its way to France. *The Mew* responded. Captain Bill Harris ordered extra coal to be loaded on to her decks and she steamed eastwards along the channel. She maintained her maximum speed for 24 hours, her boilers becoming red hot with the effort. But all to no avail. She was deemed to be unsuitable for beach work, and reluctantly made the return journey to Dartmouth – probably at a rather slower speed.

However, the following year *The Mew* was able to make a small but significant contribution to the war effort. A Royal Navy destroyer, *HMS Mistral,* got into difficulties while turning in the river in bad weather, and started drifting towards rocks near Bayards Cove. *The Mew's* captain spotted her plight, and was soon on hand to help tow the naval vessel to safety.

Between the wars, as the number of motorised cars and lorries wishing to cross the river increased, GWR decided to modify *The Mew* so that she could carry five or six vehicles as well as passengers. Her aft saloon was demolished and the deck reinforced, and at the same time the height of her funnel was increased, and an enclosed wheelhouse added. The plan was for vehicles to drive down the pontoon on to the vessel, and off again in similar fashion on the other side of the river. The elderly pontoons were strengthened, and in fact were replaced altogether a few years later once *The Mew's* success as an early prototype of the roll-on roll-off car ferry had been established.

In the years following the second world war *The Mew* continued to provide stalwart service. With the Labour government's nationalisation of the railways in 1948, she re-appeared after her annual overhaul at Devonport with her funnel shortened once more, and repainted in black and yellow, the colours of the newly created British Rail.

Although the ferry herself was still in reasonably good shape after forty years of service, there was some local dissatisfaction with the way British Rail were running the service. In 1950 Kingswear parish council wrote a disgruntled letter asking for more frequent crossings, suggesting that a passage should be made at least every twenty minutes, so presumably *The Mew* was only making the trip once or twice an hour at that time. There was considerable local ill-feeling on this issue, to the extent that the old bogey of a River Dart suspension bridge was brought up yet again, but fortunately this idea progressed no further than being a good source of argument and debate.

During the early fifties British Rail was becoming increasingly concerned about the finances of the ferry service they were obliged to run. They claimed that *The Mew* had been operating at a loss for some time. The anticipated cost of replacing the ageing vessel, an action which could not be postponed for much longer, made the economics look even worse. In an attempt to balance the books, BR doubled the fare for foot passengers to 3d, and increased other charges as well. Turning a deaf ear to the local dismay that greeted this news, two months later they announced their intention to withdraw *The Mew* and replace her with a much smaller vessel. Dismay escalated into outrage, even though it was obvious that the 46-year-old ferry was reaching the end of her useful life. It was, perhaps, the insensitive way British Rail made and announced these decisions, rather than the decisions themselves, that upset the people of Dartmouth and Kingswear. Their overall sense of dissatisfaction was not improved by the Railway's unwillingness to do anything to mark the *The Mew's* last run as the end of an era.

The townspeople finally decided that this was not good enough, took the law into their own hands, and made sure that her departure from the river on 8th October 1954 was acknowledged in the way she deserved. With 500 passengers on board, including many local dignitaries and VIPs, she made her final trip. Ships sounded their sirens, rockets flew into the sky, and crowds lining both banks of the river gave her a tumultuous send off. The band played "Hearts of Oak" as the much loved old ferry made her way out of the harbour for the last time, destined, sadly, for the breaker's yard at Plymouth. *The Mew* is still remembered fondly by older Dartmothians, and to this day her ship's bell hangs in the town museum.

Cost control was still uppermost in British Rail's mind, because the vessel they acquired to replace *The Mew* was a thirty-year-old motor launch which was not much more than half her length. She was the *Lady Elizabeth,* built in Plymouth in 1924, and named to commemorate the marriage in the previous year of Elizabeth Bowes Lyons – the late Queen Mother – to the then Duke of York, who subsequently became King George VI. *Lady Elizabeth* was chartered from the Millbrook Steamboat and Trading Company of Plymouth for a six month trial. But she was not a success, being too low and awkward to handle at the pontoons. So she returned to the Plymouth area, where she was used on both the Cawsand and Drake's Island ferry runs. However, she eventually returned to the South Hams in 1979, at the age of 55, and continued to provide pleasure for many on the Kingsbridge estuary where she operated the River Maid service for several years.

Lady Elizabeth was replaced on the Dartmouth to Kingswear crossing by *Western Belle,* a larger boat, also hired from the Millbrook Company. This gave rise to some local dissatisfaction. Why was a Plymouth vessel being used on the Dart, when local boats were available which were well capable of doing the job? For once, British Rail responded to public opinion. Millbrook's contract was terminated, and the River Dart Steamboat Company's *Seymour Castle* took over the running of the ferry service.

Perhaps by 1957 British Rail's finances had improved, because they placed an order for two new sixty foot diesel engined ferry boats with

M W Blackmore and Sons of Bideford. They were to be called *Adrian Gilbert* and *Humphrey Gilbert,* after two members of the famous local Elizabethan seafaring family who once lived at Greenway House. The official naming ceremony took place at Kingswear on 18th March 1957 and both vessels went into service immediately. They initially worked on the river for nineteen years, during which time they had three different owners.

The great expansion of Britain's railway network which took place during the middle of the 19th century lasted just over a hundred years. In the 1960s and 70s Dr. Beeching's axe fell, and many local branch lines were closed. The Goodrington to Kingswear line was one that survived, but only because of the intervention of private enterprise. In 1972 the Dart Valley Railway bought the line from British Rail. BR also offered the ferry service and the two *Gilberts* for sale, but little interest was shown and eventually Dartmouth Council picked up responsibility in order to preserve a public amenity. This was a short lived arrangement because two years later, as part of a massive reorganisation of local government across the country, the South Hams District Council came into being, and took over many of Dartmouth Council's erstwhile responsibilities, including the ferry. After a further two years the new District Council decided it no longer wished to be involved in the running of this ferry, although they chose to continue operating the nearby Lower Ferry. The pontoons were acquired by the Dart Harbour and Navigation Authority, and Dart Pleasure Craft Ltd. (DPC) were granted a licence to run the service, but the two *Gilberts* were sold.

DPC already operated a number of passenger services on the river, and started off by using two of their existing boats , *Queen Boadicea* and *Queen Boadicea II*, for ferry work. *Seafarer,* a twelve seater launch was on standby as a relief vessel.

But the Dart had not seen the last of the *Gilberts*. For a time they were both tried out on the St. Mawes ferry in Cornwall. Neither proved suitable, and they were actually sold back to British Rail, who planned to use them on their Tilbury to Gravesend ferry service on the Thames. The boats were re-engined at BR's expense but, again, were not suited to the work they were required to do.

In 1978 *Adrian Gilbert* was repurchased from the Railway by Dart Pleasure Craft, and resumed working the ferry, having been absent from the river for two years. She continued as a mainstay of the service until 1994, when she was finally sold off.

Humphrey Gilbert also eventually returned to ferry work on the Dart, but at a later date. She had a varied life during the intervening years spending some time laid up, firstly at Newhaven and then on the Thames. She returned to the west country in 1979, was renamed *Edgcumbe Belle,* and took over the Cawsand ferry run from *Lady Elizabeth.* She finally returned to the Dart in 1985, and has only recently been withdrawn from service, after forty four years of hard work.

The *Gilberts,* in spite of their chequered careers, both proved themselves to be highly successful Dart ferry boats. They were durable and reliable, and could cope with weather conditions that defeated many other vessels.

1988 saw a new arrival on the river - *Kingswear Belle* - the first twin-hulled catamaran to be used for the ferry service. She had been built in 1972 and had previously been working around the Channel Islands. Her 60 foot length and broad beam gave her excellent passenger carrying capacity. She and *Dartmouth Princess* are the two main boats operating the service today.

Between 1972 and 1999, although the ferry continued to be referred to by tradition as the Railway Ferry, there was no actual railway involvement in its management. This changed three years ago when the ferry operator, Dart Pleasure Craft, became a subsidiary company of Dart Valley Railway Plc. The historic link between railway and ferry was once again re-established. Which is appropriate, because, nearly 150 years on, one of the ferry's main tasks is still to carry railway passengers across the river from Kingswear station to Dartmouth. Today the passengers are mainly tourists – and they arrive in large numbers. In the summer months the first train of the morning from Torbay can disgorge 500 to 600 passengers at Kingswear. *Dartmouth Princess* and *Kingswear Belle*, plus any other standby boats that may be available, speed backwards and forwards to keep pace with demand.

The total number of passengers the Railway Ferry carried in 1864, its first year of operation, is not recorded, but it is reasonable to assume that it was somewhat less than the 586,384 people who were transported across the river in 2001.

THE HIGHER FERRY

In the early years of the 19th century, roads, as we know them today, were virtually non-existent in south Devon. There were paths and lanes and tracks, adequate for those on foot or horseback, but barely suitable for wheeled vehicles. But trade and commerce were growing, and the need for better roads, particularly those which made it easy for a horse drawn wagon to travel from one town to another, was growing as well. A coast road linking Exeter with Plymouth, via Teignmouth and Dartmouth, was planned. The river Teign had already been bridged, but what about the Dart?

By the early 1800s the pulling ferry between Kingswear and Bayards Cove, owned by the Fownes-Luttrell family, had been adapted so that it could carry one cart and horse across the river at a time. But this was considered to be inadequate for the level of traffic the new road was expected to carry.

John Henry Seale, whose family was prominent in Dartmouth affairs for several generations, was a great innovator. He wrote at the time:

> "To open a commodius communication across a river separating highly fertile and populous districts of the county must in all cases confer local as well as general good. This is particularly the case in the present instance.
>
> The fertility and beauty of the country on each side of the river Dart, from its mouth to Totnes, is proverbial, and within the last four years improvements have been made, and are now in progress in the roads in the districts.
>
> But these improvements are limited in their utility from the want of a more commodious union than the two common ferries of Dartmouth and Dittisham afford."

Seale asked James Rendel and John Foulston, engineer and architect respectively, to prepare a plan for bridging the Dart. They conceived the idea of a suspension bridge spanning the river at the point where it narrows between Dittisham and Greenway. Although the scheme was probably feasible technically, it immediately encountered opposition. In 1811 Greenway House had been bought by James Marwood Elton from the seafaring Gilbert family. He was appointed High Sheriff of Devon in 1815, and although he died in 1828, shortly before the bridge was proposed, his family still wielded significant influence locally. They were also the owners and operators of the Dittisham ferry, which would probably have been put out of business by the proposed new crossing. The Eltons objected strongly, and the idea of a bridge was dropped.

Rendel went back to his drawing board. Fortuitously, at this time, he had a chance meeting with a young Scottish engineer called James Nasmyth. As a teenage student in Edinburgh, Nasmyth had presented to the directors of the Forth and Clyde Navigation Co. a novel idea to control the movement of steam tugs along narrow canals. This involved laying a chain cable on the bottom of the canal, along which the tug would haul itself, thus maintaining a central course and avoiding damage to the canal banks. Nasmyth's idea was "courteously declined" by the company directors, but it provided James Rendel with the germ of an idea for a different means of crossing the Dart. Why not construct a "floating bridge" – a steam driven platform that would carry passengers and vehicles across the river guided by chains?

He took the idea to John Seale, who was impressed. Rendel went off to develop his new concept in more detail, and Seale considered his tactics for countering any possible opposition, and getting the proposal approved. He enlisted the support of Lord Morley of Saltram, an influential local figure, who was persuaded to sponsor a meeting at which the new idea of a ferry could be debated openly by all interested parties. The meeting was duly held at the Castle Hotel on 3rd October 1829 – although the noble lord himself unfortunately had to proffer his apologies for absence, having been "attacked suddenly by the gout". In his absence, Mr. George Stanley Carey of Follaton was invited to take the chair, and he duly asked Mr. Rendel to address the meeting. The engineer described his design for the proposed new floating bridge, and also provided estimates of the costs of its construction and operation, including the necessary new roads on both sides of the river.

Rendel's presentation was received with general enthusiasm. Even Mr. Edward Elton of Greenway sent a message to the meeting saying he would not stand in the way of this proposal. Nevertheless, several of those present also stressed the importance of detailed plans being formally approved by all organisations that held an interest in the river, including the Duchy of Cornwall, which actually owns the waters of the river Dart.

A committee was formed to take matters forward. An Act of Parliament was required to authorise the project and its financing, and a petition to raise the enabling parliamentary bill was presented to the House of Commons on 17th February 1830. At this point the project began to falter. In May, during the second reading of the bill, it was opposed by the Duchy of Cornwall, which had not previously raised any objections. The Duchy claimed that the new ferry would interfere with the navigation of the river, and infringe its rights.

Immediately, more latent opposition began to emerge, not least from the Holdsworths – a family of considerable power and influence in Dartmouth. The Holdsworths and Seales were traditionally antagonistic towards one another, and were likely to adopt contrary views on most issues of local importance.

Rumours abounded that the new scheme was doomed. An alternative solution of a suspension bridge, this time from the centre of Dartmouth across to Kingswear, was proposed yet again.

But John Seale and his fellow supporters were not to be deterred. They called upon the Master Attendant of Plymouth Dockyard to make an independent assessment of the Duchy's claims, and he concluded that the presence of the ferry would not interfere with navigation on the river. The Duchy accordingly withdrew its objection, and without this main foundation, the rest of the opposition collapsed as well.

The Floating Bridge Act was no trivial piece of legislation. It contained 100 clauses spread over 46 pages of finely printed legal language, and aimed to cover every conceivable eventuality that might ever affect the

13. Floating bridge No. 2 in 1856, still driven by "horse power".

14. Raleigh Estates new floating bridge – the third – in 1876.

15. Floating bridge No. 5 makes the crossing to Dartmouth in 1912.

16. The Higher Ferry on a busy summer's day in 1950.

installation and operation of the bridge. It was officially entitled:

> "An Act for establishing a Floating Bridge over the Harbour of *Dartmouth,* from or near to *Lower Sandquay Point* to *Old Rock* in the County of *Devon,* and for building Quays and Landing Places, and for making Roads and Approaches thereto, with Branches therefrom."

The preamble to the Act explained to parliament that the Bridge –

> "…will be of great Advantage and Accommodation to the Proprietors and Occupiers of Lands in the Neighbourhood of the said Bridge, and the several adjacent Parishes, and will facilitate the Communication between the various Seaports and Towns situate on the Southern Coast of the said County, and will in many other Respects be of great public Utility…"

The proposed legislation was debated and approved. The Act received the Royal Assent on 17th June 1830, and the Dartmouth Floating Bridge Company was duly formed.

Although this event was a cause for much celebration, it would subsequently become apparent that some of the detailed provisions of the Act were much too restrictive, and severely limited the Company's ability to run the bridge at a profit.

But these were problems that would only emerge at a later date. In the summer of 1830 there was universal enthusiasm as all the essential preparatory work got under way.

In January 1831 notices appeared in the local newspapers inviting prospective contractors to tender for all the necessary construction work, and Isaac Blackburn of Turnchapel, Plymouth was commissioned to build the new ferry. The vessel was 40 feet long and 30 feet wide, and it had two hulls, like a catamaran. Lengthwise it was divided into three sections. The two outer sections provided accommodation for carriages, people and animals. The centre section was occupied by a 4 hp steam engine with two boilers, which were to be used on alternate weeks. The engine powered a capstan which drove two toothed wheels. These engaged with forged iron chains which stretched across the river and were anchored to large granite blocks on either shore. As the wheels turned the ferry slowly hauled itself along the chains from bank to bank.

While this unusual ferry was being constructed in Plymouth, preparations for its arrival were being made on both sides of the Dart. On 28th April 1831 John Seale's daughter ceremoniously laid a foundation stone, which, incidentally, referred rather grandiosely to the inauguration of the "flying bridge" rather than the "floating bridge".

Roads were built from the Ship-in-Dock public house to Lower Sandquay on the west bank, and from Old Rock at Lower Noss Point up to Brixham Cross at Hill Head on the east. Each road terminated at a new slipway into the river.

There doesn't seem to be a conclusive record of just how much the whole project actually cost. When Rendel made his presentation to the meeting at the Castle Hotel, he estimated costs of £2550 for the ferry and its machinery, and a further £2950 for building the approach roads. By February 1830 – four months later, and at the time the draft bill was first being introduced to the House of Commons – he produced a revised estimate of £3650 for the whole project. Perhaps this latter figure was based more on what Parliament would find acceptable, rather than a realistic view of the expected cost. What is certain, is that the total sum actually spent significantly exceeded the £4000 of capital authorised by the Floating Bridge Act, and additional funds had to be raised by way of mortgage. This was to cause more problems in the years to come.

Nevertheless, all the preparations were eventually completed. The new ferry arrived in the river, and the people of Dartmouth awaited the official opening with eager anticipation. They were not to be disappointed.

Just after mid day on Friday, 19th August 1831 a procession of dignitaries, some in carriages, some on horseback, wound its way through cheering crowds down the road from Hill Head to the slipway at Lower Noss. There they boarded the floating bridge, and the "puffing giant" – as it was named by the contemporary author, Valentine Butteris – clanked its way across the river for the first time. The procession, made up of some sixty carriages, two hundred horses, and even more pedestrians, was so long that it took four hours and numerous crossings to transport everybody to the Dartmouth side. There they were received by more crowds and bands, and eventually made their way to Mount Boone House, the home of the Seale family, where an elegant reception was enjoyed.

After its inaugural day of glory, the floating bridge settled in to the routine of daily operations. It carried a crew of two, one man on the bridge, and one to attend to the engine. They were paid two shillings (10p) and three shillings (15p) per day respectively. The daily coal consumption of the engine was six bushels, which added a further five shillings (25p) to operating expenses.

The floating bridge, as a semi-experimental engineering project, was deemed to be a success. But in those early days, travelling on it was not without its hazards. In February 1833 a letter to John Seale, then resident in London, from his wife, Paulina, contained an account of a homeward journey following a grand ball in Dartmouth:

> "At about 2 o'clock in the morning the Buller party retired, and all four carriages got onto the Bridge as they had done in coming. The wind which had been blowing extremely hard all night seemed a little abated, but when they had reached rather more than half way across, it suddenly changed and a most tremendous squall from the north west impelled the Bridge with such force that the right side got off too far from the hard, and the carriages on that side could not be landed. The two other carriages came out safely, but with much difficulty the Ladies were conveyed

> from the carriage on the right side, which was filled with water, to the other, and proceeded to Lupton. The people were then obliged to put the Bridge off again with the two empty carriages, intending to cross with them again, but had not gone far when water rushed into the Bridge with such violence through the chain holes that they were compelled to force it back to shore with all the power of the engine, and it grounded safely. But the engineer told me this morning that had they lost a moment it would have sunk in the middle of the river. The unhappy Conservatives must have been in a very uncomfortable predicament, for the lights were extinguished by the water dashing over the carriages, and total darkness was added to their other misfortunes."

John Seale was a staunch Whig, and was MP for Dartmouth at that time, which accounts for his wife's rather ill-concealed glee at the troubles of the Conservative Buller family.

In August of the same year the floating bridge carried its first royal passenger. The 14-year-old Princess Victoria – later to be Queen – was travelling from Plymouth to Torquay on the royal yacht with her mother, the Duchess of Kent,. She had, however, suffered from such sea-sickness that the yacht made an unscheduled stop at Dartmouth. Having had some time to recover, the Duchess and the Princess were taken for a tour of the harbour in their barge, and then, having borrowed a carriage from the Seales, they crossed the river on the bridge and completed their journey to Torquay by road.

There was a steady flow of less important travellers using the new ferry in its early years, but perhaps not as many as James Rendel had assumed when he originally forecast the finances of the enterprise. Once the tolls for various categories of passenger had been set – one penny per person, two pence each for cattle, and three pence for a horse – Rendel had made detailed estimates of the daily traffic he thought the ferry would carry, and the income it would generate as a result. Not surprisingly, but perhaps over optimistically, his sums showed that the operation would be profitable.

In the event, the floating bridge struggled to break even, let alone make a profit. The way the Floating Bridge Act had been drawn up did not help the situation. The tolls that the ferry owners could charge were written in to the Act itself, and although specific provision was made for the owners to *reduce* these charges, no provision was made for them to be *increased*.

In addition the Floating Bridge Company was required to make a very generous payment of £60 a year to John Fownes-Luttrell, the owner of the Lower Ferry, to compensate him for loss of trade. But worst of all, the Act specifically directed that all Royal Mail traffic should be carried free of charge, even though the Post Office had previously been paying Fownes-Luttrell £15 a year for this service.

Lord Morley pressed the Postmaster General, Lord Lichfield, for a more equitable arrangement, but for a long time was met with persistent refusals, the Post Office relying on the letter of the law as enshrined in the Act.

The situation was made worse by the Post Office's continual demands for an improved service. By 1835 the bridge was required to be in operation for eighteen hours a day and had to be readily available to carry the mail coach across the river whenever it appeared – still for free. The impact on the bridge's finances was unacceptable, and Lord Morley threatened to close down the ferry altogether. So, after four years of intransigence, the Post Office finally accepted the unfairness of the situation, and grudgingly agreed to pay the Company £50 per year.

But it was too little, too late. The bridge was continuing to run at a loss, and economies had to be made. In 1836 the decision was taken to do away with the costly steam engine and revert to a more basic form of horse power – literally two horses working a treadmill amidships to turn the capstan. Tales were told locally of the horses being blind, and badly treated as well, but whether these were true or not, the new arrangement worked reasonably well, and was certainly a lot less expensive than a steam engine.

Lord Morley died in 1840, and his death was followed by that of John

Seale – by then Sir John – in 1844. The mortgage on the ferry transferred to John's son, Sir Henry Paul Seale, who also became its effective proprietor.

Finance was not the owner's only worry. There is no doubt that in it's early years the floating bridge was a bit vulnerable to extreme weather conditions. Following the Buller family's unfortunate experience in 1833, the bridge suffered its first sinking two years later when it foundered on its mooring during a heavy gale. It was out of action for ten days. A similar disaster occurred twenty years later in September 1855. But by then the vessel – still the original – had been in operation for twenty four years, and inspections soon confirmed that it was beyond repair. With no replacement available, the Higher Ferry ceased operation.

This was not popular with the local community. In spite of its problems it had become, over the years, an important part of the area's transport infrastructure, essential to the carrying of the mails, and also to a number of local businesses, which were considerably inconvenienced by its absence

The original Act of 1830 required the bridge to be in continuous operation. A group of dissatisfied tradespeople, led by Thomas Lakeman, a Brixham brewer, accused the Company of failing to meet its legal obligations. They issued a writ of Mandamus (- an order to a public officer to carry out his duty) directing the Company to show just cause for not restoring the service. The net effect was for the Floating Bridge Company to be declared insolvent, leaving Sir Henry Seale, as mortgagee, to pick up the pieces.

It seems as if Sir Henry responded positively to this challenge because he requested William Kelly, a Dartmouth shipbuilder, to draw up plans, specifications and costings for a new bridge, and subsequently authorised the construction work to proceed.

Nevertheless it was over a year before the new ferry commenced operation on 31st October 1856. It was some thirty tons lighter than Rendel's original vessel, but retained the principle of a horse driven capstan, which had previously proved to be both effective and economic.

After another eleven years, perhaps the ferry's finances were on a firmer footing, as the decision was taken to reintroduce steam power, and dispense with the old horse treadmill.

This was probably achieved by adapting the existing vessel, rather than building a completely new one, because during the next few years the ferry seemed to be showing signs of age. On Christmas Eve 1871 she once again sank at her moorings, and it was reported that she had been leaking for some time previously. There was immediate concern for the chargehand who normally slept on board, but on that occasion he had fortuitously decided to spend the night ashore! Then, the following year, one of the chains broke leaving the ferry stranded in mid stream, and the cattle on board had to swim to the river bank .

1873 saw a change in ownership. Sir Henry Seale decided to sell much of his property and business interests, and this included the floating bridge. The purchaser was the Raleigh Estates Trustees. They took over responsibility for the ferry, and tried to keep the service running with Seale's elderly vessel. But problems abounded, and they finally abandoned their attempts after a year. It seems likely that Raleigh Estates then had a mind to dispose of the ferry, but could find no prospective purchaser willing to take it on. Eventually they placed an order for a new ferry with Willoughbys of Plymouth, but she did not arrive on the Dart until 1876, by which time there had been no Higher Ferry operating for two years.

The new vessel was 52 feet long and 28 feet wide, with 20 foot loading ramps, or prows as they were called, at each end. Horse drawn vehicles were carried in the centre "roadway", and there were passenger cabins on both sides. She was powered by twin steam engines, and could speed across the river in three minutes. The Chronicle was suitably impressed, but expressed surprise, and indeed dismay, that the recommencement of the ferry service would be further delayed because essential repair work to the slipways and approaches had not been carried out while the ferry was under construction. The paper commented somewhat pointedly – "If the traffic which has been so long diverted is to be restored and increased , it will only be by efficient management and regular periods of departure".

It would seem as if Raleigh Estates rose to the challenge. This new floating bridge, the third, performed well and uneventfully for quite a number of years. But in the 1890s she too was beginning to deteriorate. As ever, her owners were reluctant to stand the cost of a replacement, and postponed taking a decision about this for as long as possible. By 1895 it would appear that the old vessel was spending more time out of service than it was working, and Raleigh Estates had to face up to the inevitable. They placed an order for a new floating bridge with Philip and Son, whose shipyard at the time was still at Sandquay, before its removal to Noss. This was Philip's first direct involvement with the Higher Ferry, but started a relationship which has continued over a hundred years to the present day.

Raleigh Estates thought they might be able to partly cover the cost of the new ferry by finding a buyer for the old one, but it was in such a dilapidated condition that its proposed sale attracted little interest.

The new Philip's vessel commenced operation in 1896. She was 47 feet long and 25 feet wide – a little smaller than her predecessor – but was substantially upgraded on power with a 90 hp steam engine built by Lees Anderson and Co. For the first time the chains ran outside the vessel rather than internally, but perhaps the most important innovation for passengers was that they no longer had to mingle with cattle, which were now confined in a separate pen.

Since its inception the Higher Ferry had been operated by its owners. But in 1899 Raleigh Estates decided to contract the service out, and a lease was awarded to a Mr. Percy of London, who was already running ferries at Penzance, Exeter, and the Menai Straits.

A few years later the floating bridge played an important role in the modernisation of Kingswear. Although Dartmouth had enjoyed gas light since the middle of the nineteenth century, a pipeline had never been laid across the river, and Kingswear had had to make do with a few oil streetlights. But in 1903 it was decided that the east bank village should have the luxury of electricity. Special drums were installed on a lighter which was attached to the side of the ferry, and the new cable was wound off them on to the river bed as the two vessels slowly crossed the river in tandem. A few days later on the 22nd October, after all the necessary connections had been made, Kingswear was illuminated with such brilliance that its inhabitants celebrated in the streets.

But perhaps this event was the highlight of the fourth floating bridge's career. At some time in the next five years Mr. Percy must have disappeared off the scene, because by 1908 the ferry, although only twelve years old, was lying derelict and abandoned off Sandquay. Raleigh Estates had rather half-heartedly introduced a small rowing ferry as a substitute, which did little to quell the growing levels of local dissatisfaction at the absence of the bridge.

The floating bridge did not in fact operate at all between 1908 and 1912. It was clear that Raleigh Estates had lost both enthusiasm for, and interest in the ferry, and responded to criticism by threatening to close it down altogether. The situation generated considerable local concern. The town councils of Dartmouth, Brixham, Torquay and Paignton, and even Devon County Council were all involved in discussions as to how the service could be restored – each one hoping that one of the others would volunteer to take it on. None did.

Eventually Mr. John Williams of Devonport, who was already the owner of the Torpoint chain ferry, stepped in and agreed to buy the ferry rights from Raleigh Estates for £265.

Mr Williams requested Messrs Rogers and Co. of Cremyll shipyard, Plymouth to construct a new ferry at a cost of £1000.

Having made this investment Mr. Williams, not unreasonably, asked Brixham Borough Council for some help in repairing the road down to the ferry from Hill Head. They somewhat grudgingly agreed to make their road roller available to him at a cost of one pound five shillings a day – provided it was not required for other Council work.

The new floating bridge – No. 5 – was launched in Plymouth during

September 1912, towed round to Dartmouth by the tug *Venture* in October, and went into service in November. After an absence of four years, the Higher Ferry was back in action.

Her length of 77 feet exceeded any of her predecessors, and she was guided across the river by wire ropes wound around drums, rather than the chains used previously.

Only two years after the ferry restarted, war broke out in Europe and the world began to change. As more and more of the country's male population became involved in active service, it became difficult to find sufficient men to operate and maintain the vessel. At the same time, the ferry was being required to carry an increasing volume of military vehicles and personnel, which the original Act decreed must travel free of charge. Not surprisingly, the financial situation once again became precarious, and Mr. Williams had to borrow money to keep going.

Matters were made worse when the ferry was damaged during a particularly violent storm in 1916 which caused havoc throughout the harbour. The ferry was torn from its moorings and ended up aground on the Kingswear shore, along with a number of other vessels. She was recovered but, no doubt, at some extra cost to Mr. Williams.

He nevertheless continued to own and operate the ferry for the remainder of the War years, and for some time afterwards. But in 1920 the floating bridge, together with its slipways and approach roads, were put up for sale by auction. What appears to be the only bid was one of £500 from Philip's. This was less than Williams' reserve price, and he withdrew the sale. This tactic proved to be successful as Philip's then returned with a significantly improved offer of £1900, and the sale was duly completed on 28th July 1920.

Although the floating bridge acquired by Philip's was only eight years old, she was withdrawn from service while a new ferry was being built in Philip's own shipyard at Noss. Perhaps a lack of proper maintenance during the war years contributed to her premature demise. In any case, travellers once again had to make do without the Higher Ferry, which again ceased operation for a period of eighteen months before the new vessel was ready for service.

Philip's floating bridge No. 6 was the first to be driven by paddle wheels, and she had a greater passenger carrying capacity than ever before. Her eighteen foot wide roadway could simultaneously accommodate four charabancs, which were becoming an increasingly common sight in the area as tourism became more popular.

But perhaps the most interesting feature of this new ferry is the fact that it was powered by the engines originally installed in No. 4 – the first one built by Philip's some twenty four years previously. This was the vessel that had lain abandoned on the mud after Raleigh Estates discontinued the Higher Ferry service in 1908. Presumably, the engines, at least, must have been retrieved by Philip's and stored for later use. The quality of Victorian mechanical engineering was so good that it was not unusual for marine engines to be used in more than one vessel.

The re-commencement of the ferry service, after an absence of eighteen months, was awaited with such eagerness, that Philip's decided to start operating it before the construction of the new floating bridge was finally complete. For the first few weeks, until its machinery was fully operational, the bridge was propelled across the river attached to a steam launch.

Although rushed in to service, this latest vessel proved to be both reliable and durable. She faithfully ploughed backwards and forwards across the river for forty years, until she was eventually replaced in 1960.

During this time she carried many famous and distinguished passengers. Ferrymen of the post war years could remember carrying many show business personalities such as Cary Grant, Sid James and Kenneth More. And in 1946 a royal passenger was once again on board. Princess Elizabeth, who had met her then fiancé, Prince Philip, at Britannia Royal Naval College some eight years previously, was involved in sea ranger activities on the Dart that year, and it is believed that she used the ferry to cross the river on at least one occasion.

But, inevitably, from time to time the floating bridge was involved in less happy events as well. One such occurred not long after ferry No. 6 had gone into service. A herd of cattle was being transported across the river, when one nervous bullock managed to break loose and plunged down an eight foot drop to land immediately in front of the boiler. Extracting the live animal in mid-stream was not feasible, and its presence in the stokehold made it impossible to fuel the boiler, so the vessel was immobilised. Eventually a vet had to be called out from Dartmouth to put the poor beast out of its misery. The carcass was hoisted clear – and normal service was resumed.

Vehicles have been lost from the ferry on a number of occasions, and for a variety of reasons. But, fortunately, only one fatality has ever occurred. This was a Mr. Pearn who, although disabled, drove a van around the villages selling fish. He was a regular user of the ferry, but on one day in 1923 he drove his van on to the vessel and did not stop. The vehicle shot over the far prow, into the river, where it immediately sank. Whether poor Mr Pearn had had a heart attack or stroke nobody knows, but sadly he died before anybody could rescue him.

July 1960 saw the arrival on the river of floating bridge No. 7, which still operates the service today. Constructed by Philip and Son at Noss, she is the first Higher Ferry vessel to carry the name of her constructor, owner and operator – *Philip.* With capacity to carry up to eighteen vehicles, she is the largest ferry so far. With *Philip's* launch, the 130 year era of horse and steam powered ferries came to an end. She is powered by two big diesel-electric engines, and her paddle wheels can be controlled independently of one another, which gives the captain much greater flexibility in coping with any situation that might arise.

However, this improved manoeuvrability was probably of little assistance when one of the most costly "car overboard" incidents occurred quite soon after *Philip* was launched. One Sunday morning a Bentley was driven on to the ferry. The owner stepped out to admire the view, but omitted to apply the handbrake. Quietly the expensive motor car slipped into the river. Frantic but unsuccessful efforts were made to keep it afloat, and the vehicle sank to the mud 25 feet below the surface. It was subsequently located by a diver from the Naval College, and recovered by the harbourmaster, but whether it was ever again restored to running order is not known. There is a rumour, unconfirmed, that the owner of the car was Richard Dimbleby, the well known broadcaster, whose family still holiday frequently at Dittisham.

Apart from cars overboard, the other hazard for ferries such as the floating bridge is the breakage of one, or both, of the guiding chains or wires. Fortunately this, too, is a rare event, and generally only happens in extremely severe weather conditions. The first occurrence was in 1872. There was another in the late 1940s when the ferry was battling across a strong ebb tide and a north easterly gale. One cable parted, and the strain on the second was so great that it gave way as well. An emergency call went out to the Philip's tug, but by the time it arrived the ferry, by then making increasingly rapid progress downstream, had decided to drop her emergency anchor.

The most recent cable breakage was in 1984, when the ferry again broke loose, and was swept downstream. She collided with twelve yachts before she was halted by her anchor in the middle of the river. Unfortunately, on this occasion one of the vehicles on board was an ambulance carrying a sick woman to hospital. The floating bridge was eventually towed to the shore, but the Lower Ferry float had to be summoned to help unload the vehicles.

But these dramas are rare indeed. In the main, *Philip* trundles uneventfully to and fro across the Dart each day, as she has done with only an occasional break for the last forty two years. During that time she has been repaired, modified and improved. But she still travels some 12,000 miles in a year, and provides locals and tourists alike with an essential, but pleasurable step in their journeys.

POSTSCRIPT

Many centuries have past since our early ancestors first attempted to paddle their way from one shore to the other. Today we have three modern ferries which carry thousands of people and vehicles across the river every year. And yet there are still debates about the adequacy of these services in the 21st century.

If you are a tourist, arriving in Dartmouth via the floating bridge, little has changed in concept since engineer Rendel's original design of 1830, and it is part of what you came for. It epitomises a more relaxed, leisurely and old world way of life - a complete contrast to the frenetic bustle of urban living from which you have just escaped.

If you live and work in Dartmouth, and perhaps have a need to use the ferry twice a day every day, an hour's wait to cross the river in the summer months can be pretty frustrating.

Should a suspension bridge be built? It has been proposed often enough in the past. And it would certainly speed up the movement of road traffic, deemed to be so important to the economic health of modern society.

But there is no doubt that a new bridge would fundamentally change the appearance, and even the character of the town. The ferries would go – and perhaps also so would the tourists, who are now unarguably essential to Dartmouth's existence. They come to the town because of what it is today, and what it has been over centuries gone by. Achieving the fastest possible crossing of the river is not high on their lists of priorities.

To bridge or not to bridge? A question for future generations to answer.

REFERENCES

Blackhurst D., *Philip and Son Ltd.*
Clammer R. and Kittridge A., *Passenger Steamers of the River Dart and Kingsbridge Estuary.*
Collinson D., *The Chronicles of Dartmouth.*
Freeman R., *Dartmouth and Its Neighbours.*
Holgate M., *Along the River Dart.*
Langley M. and Small E., *Estuary and River Ferries of South West England*
Perkins K., *Origins of the Dartmouth Floating Bridge.*
Potts C., *The Newton Abbott to Kingswear Railway.*
Russell P. and York G., *Kingswear and Neighbourhood.*
Smart I., *The Dartmouth Harbour Papers.*

- and with help from

Tony Eden
Ray Freeman
Wally Fleet
Jan Cowling
Basil Cowling
Dave Coysh
Derek Blackhurst
Malcolm Pope
Kerry Southern
Dart Pleasure Craft Ltd
Dartmouth Museum
Dartmouth Library
South Hams District Council
The West Countries Study Library
The Seale Family Papers

Previous Publications by the Dartmouth History Research Group.

1. The Holdsworth and Newman Families in Dartmouth. by Ray Freeman
2. Dartmouth Cottage Hospital. A History by Dr. W. G. Keane
3. The Dartmouth Residences of Thomas Newcomen and his Family. by I. H. Smart.
4. Brownstone: A Devon Farm Through Seven Centuries. by Ray Freeman.
5. The Guildhalls of Dartmouth. by I. H. Smart
6. The Free French in Kingswear. by Tony Higgins
7. The Newcomen Memorials in Dartmouth. by I. H. Smart.
8. The Story of Warfleet. by Ray Freeman.
9. Oldstone . The Story of a Ruined Mansion. by Ursula Dimes.
10. Wrecks off the South Devon Coast. by Tony Aylmer.
11. We Remember D-Day. Compiled by Ray Freeman.
12. A Wrens-Eye View of Wartime Dartmouth. Compiled by Ray Freeman.
13. The Development of Dartmouth Millpond. by I. H. Smart.
15. The Newcomen Road . by I. H. Smart
16. Memories of War. Compiled by Ray Freeman
17. River Dart Pilotage. By Dave Griffiths
18. Dartmouth Industry and Banking 1795 to 1925. By I H Smart
19. Sir Thomas Wilton JP CA. A Biography. By Dr T N P N Wilton
20. Operation Fahrenheit. By Michel Guillou
21. Wadstray House. By Irene O'Shea
22. A Dittisham Boy's Story. By Ewart Hutchins
23. The Secret War from the River Dart. By Lloyd Bott
24. Hawley's Fortalice, Dartmouth's First Castle. By Terry Edwards
25. The History of the Castle Hotel, Dartmouth. By Ray Freeman
26. William Veale, Master Mariner, 1791 - 1867. By Linda King
27. The Torbay Paint Company. By Bridget Howard
28. Sportspeople of Dartmouth. By Alan Coles
29. John Flavel, A Famous Dartmouth Puritan. By Freeman

Available from:

The Dartmouth Museum, The Butterwalk, Dartmouth, Devon. TQ6 9PZ

The Harbour Bookshop, 12 Fairfax Place, Dartmouth, Devon, TQ6 9AE
Tel. and Fax. (01803) 832448. Overseas orders welcome.

Compass Books, 17 Newcomen Road, Dartmouth, Devon, TQ6 9BN
Tel. 01803 835915 Overseas orders welcome.